CW00376406

SLOW FOOD

SLOW FOOD

From old-fashioned soups to casseroles, stews and perfect puddings and pies: taking the time to create authentic home-cooked food with maximum taste

Jenni Fleetwood

LORENZ BOOKS

This edition is published by Lorenz Books

Lorenz Books is an imprint of Anness Publishing Limited
Hermes House, 88–89 Blackfriars Road, London SE1 8HA
tel. 020 7401 2077; fax 020 7633 9499
www.lorenzbooks.com; www.annesspublishing.com

If you like the images in this book and would like to investigate using them for publishing, promotions or advertising, please visit our website www.practicalpictures.com for more information.

UK agent: The Manning Partnership Ltd, 6 The Old Dairy, Melcombe Road, Bath BA2 3LR
tel. 01225 478 444; fax 01225 478 440; sales@manning-partnership.co.uk

UK distributor: Grantham Book Services Ltd, Isaac Newton Way, Alma Park Industrial Estate, Grantham, Lincs NG31 9SD; tel. 01476 541080; fax 01476 541061; orders@gbs.tbs-ltd.co.uk

North American agent/distributor: National Book Network, 4501 Forbes Boulevard, Suite 200, Lanham, MD 20706; tel. 301 459 3366; fax 301 429 5746; www.nbnbooks.com

Australian agent/distributor: Pan Macmillan Australia, Level 18, St Martins Tower, 31 Market St, Sydney, NSW 2000; tel. 1300 135 113; fax 1300 135 103; customer.service@macmillan.com.au

New Zealand agent/distributor: David Bateman Ltd, 30 Tarndale Grove, Off Bush Road, Albany, Auckland; tel. (09) 415 7664; fax (09) 415 8892

A CIP catalogue record for this book is available from the British Library.

PUBLISHER: Joanna Lorenz
MANAGING EDITOR: Judith Simons
SENIOR EDITOR: Sarah Ainley
COPY EDITOR: Jane Bamforth
DESIGNER: Louise Clements
RECIPES: Mridula Baljekar, Ghillie Basan, Maxine Clark, Matthew Drennan, Jenni Fleetwood, Brian Glover, Lucy Knox, Keith Richmond and Rena Salaman
PHOTOGRAPHY: Martin Brigdale, Nicki Dowey, Craig Robertson and William Lingwood
PRODUCTION CONTROLLER: Pedro Nelson

10 9 8 7 6 5 4 3 2 1

Previously published as *Slow Cooking*

NOTES

Bracketed terms are intended for American readers.

For all recipes, quantities are given in both metric and imperial measures and, where appropriate, measures are also given in standard cups and spoons. Follow one set, but not a mixture, because they are not interchangeable.

Standard spoon and cup measures are level.
1 tsp = 5ml, 1 tbsp = 15ml, 1 cup = 250ml|8fl oz

Australian standard tablespoons are 20ml. Australian readers should use 3 tsp in place of 1 tbsp for measuring small quantities of gelatine, flour, salt, etc.

American pints are 16fl oz/2 cups. American readers should use 20fl oz/2.5 cups in place of 1 pint when measuring liquids.

Medium (US large) eggs are used unless otherwise stated.

Front cover shows Chunky Tomato Soup with Noodles – for recipe see page 20.

SOUPS

CASSEROLES AND STEWS

OVEN ROASTS AND BAKES

PUDDINGS AND DESSERTS

CONTENTS

cook it slow

What do nourishing soups, hearty stews and casseroles, robust roasts and moreish desserts have in common? They are all favourite comfort foods, they all benefit from lengthy cooking, and they are all as much of a pleasure to serve as they are to eat.

The common theme of the dishes brought together in this collection is minimum fuss for maximum flavour. Cooking a meal where the bulk of the cooking is done in one pot is hugely liberating. All that is needed is the initial preparation, and then the cook can relax, secure in the knowledge that the food is taking care of itself.

Serving a choice of side dishes with these recipes is largely unnecessary as, if vegetables are not included in the dish, they are generally not needed. This gives you the perfect excuse for offering only the essential accompaniments. After all, simple foods are rarely any less satisfying.

Slow-cooked dishes tend to be fairly undemanding, and are not likely to spoil if they are not eaten the moment they are ready. Some, like curries and casseroles, actually improve if made the day before.

CHUNKY TOMATO SOUP WITH NOODLES

ROAST CHICKEN WITH POTATOES

STICKY MAPLE AND PECAN STEAMED PUD

This wonderful book offers practical advice on slow cooking, from suitable equipment to the basic cooking techniques, along with four fabulous chapters of mouthwatering recipes

SOUP IT UP

Few dishes give more satisfaction than a good home-made soup, and with so many soup recipes cooked slowly over a low heat, it is worth devoting a whole chapter to them. Included here are classic recipes, such as Jewish chicken noodle soup and aromatic fish bouillabaisse. Bacon and chickpea soup, served with tortilla chips, and chunky tomato soup with noodles are pure comfort foods, while Toulouse sausages and borlotti beans are combined to make a very tasty and substantial meal.

BRAISE, SIMMER AND STEW

This chapter brings together the best of stove-top casseroles and stews. Some, such as the Moroccan tagine of beef with peas and saffron are based on a cooking style that has ancient origins but is now at the forefront of contemporary cooking. Two very different Indian curry dishes are other such examples. From Italy comes a satisfying pasta sauce made from tomatoes and chorizo, and from Greece there is chicken simmered in red wine and spices. A succulent veal, beer and caramelized onion dish from England completes the line-up.

ROAST AND BAKE

When it comes to winter warmers there is nothing quite like a baked hotpot with dumplings or a steaming beef pudding with a thick suet crust, and this chapter offers two of the best. For celebration dinners or lazy Sundays, a meat roast is an easy meal. For a new take on the traditional method, put chicken and potatoes in the same roasting pan and drizzle with lemon juice, or try a pot-roast of pork with cider sauce: the flavours are truly magical. For a side dish or vegetarian main course, bake a gratin of leek, squash and tomato.

PERFECT PUDDINGS

Steamed puddings and fruit crumbles, served with hot custard or thick double cream, are some of life's greatest pleasures. And if it's pure decadence you're after, look no further than this version of bread and butter pudding made with pains au chocolat...

equipment

It is always worth choosing cookware with care and investing in practical good quality pieces that will last. Slow cooking techniques do not require specialist equipment especially, but you should always use an appropriate piece of equipment for the task.

POTS AND PANS

For one-pot slow cooking, you will need a large pan with a heavy base, which will conduct the heat evenly and help to prevent the food from scorching should you inadvertently allow the liquid to get too low. For long, slow cooking, cast-iron pans coated in vitreous enamel are ideal, as they can be used both on the stove and in the oven.

CASSEROLES

Choose a casserole that is big enough to serve six, even if you usually cook for four. This will give you plenty of room for stirring the contents without risking splashes and scalds. The ideal pot will be one that can be used on top of the stove as well as inside the oven, so that if you do need to do any pre-cooking, or if cooking juices need to be reduced by boiling, you will not need to transfer the food to a second, ovenproof container. If you buy several casseroles, try to vary the shapes and sizes. For cooking a whole chicken, for example, an oval dish is more useful than a round dish.

Take a look at the handles, too. It is important that they are easy to grasp, and that they do not become so hot that they are liable to burn you, even when you are using oven gloves. Appearance will obviously be a consideration, since you will often be serving straight from the casserole, but consider the practical aspects too.

The most versatile casseroles are flameproof and so can be used on top of the stove and under the grill (broiler), as well as in the oven.

BAKING DISHES

There are plenty of recipes that benefit from being cooked in large, shallow dishes, from oven-roasted vegetables to layered potato bakes. Buy several different shapes, bearing in mind the shape of your oven.

POTS AND PANS

CASSEROLES

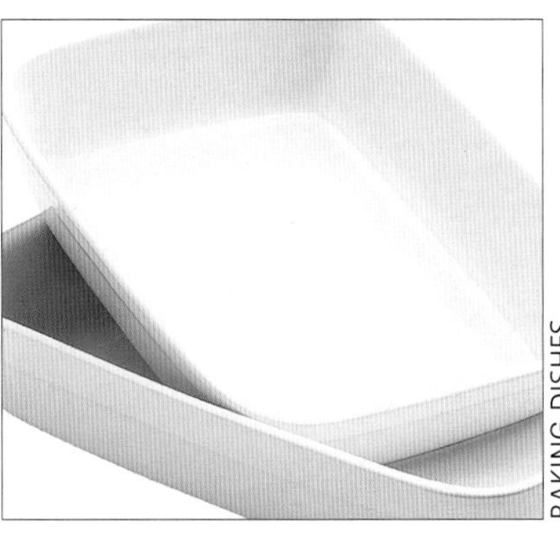

BAKING DISHES

GLAZED EARTHENWARE

TRADITIONAL TAGINES

STOCKPOT

Having two rectangular dishes that will fit side by side can be a real bonus if you want to cook one meal for serving immediately and another for the freezer.

GLAZED EARTHENWARE BAKEWARE

These dishes can often be put straight into a hot oven, or used under a hot grill for browning. They are also suitable for use in the freezer. Unlike clay pots and porous earthenware, they do not need to be soaked in water before use, and they will not absorb food flavours or become discoloured with use.

TAGINES

This traditional North African cooking pot consists of a large, shallow base and a tall, conical lid. The dish that is cooked in it is also known as a tagine. The food is placed in the base. As it cooks, steam rises from the food and is trapped in the lid, keeping the food moist throughout the cooking time.

Tagines are traditionally made from glazed brown earthenware, sometimes with a slightly rounded base. They come in a range of sizes, from small individual tagines to family-sized ones that measure at least 20cm|8in across. There is also a modern version, with a heavy, cast-iron base and a glazed earthenware lid. Unlike the traditional tagine, which can be used only in the oven, or on a barbecue whose coals have been dowsed with sand, the cast-iron design can also be used on top of the stove. This is very convenient, since it means that onions, vegetables and other ingredients, such as meat and poultry, can be browned in the base before the lid is fitted and the tagine is placed in the oven. Some glazed earthenware tagines can be used directly on top of the stove over a low heat, but it is best to use a heat diffuser; always check the manufacturer's instructions for your particular model as misuse can cause irreparable damage.

STOCKPOT

A large, deep pan for making stock and cooking larger cuts of meat is an extremely useful piece of kitchen equipment. Heavy-duty stainless steel pans will last a lifetime. Look for a pan with a small metal handle on both sides, then it will double as a huge ovenproof casserole, ideal for roasts and bakes as well as stove-top dishes.

slow cooking techniques

Mastering a few basic techniques will make for greater efficiency in the kitchen, especially when preparing the ingredients for slow-cook dishes. Many of the recipes in this collection need little attention while cooking, but it is always important to follow the instructions as regards temperature, stirring and checking the liquid content of the dish.

STEWING, BRAISING AND CASSEROLING MEAT

These are long, slow and moist methods of cooking and they can be used either on top of the stove or in the oven. For stewing and braising, the meat is cut into cubes, while for casseroling it is cut into thick steaks or slices. After tossing the meat in seasoned flour, it is browned over a high heat in a heavy pan or casserole on top of the stove to seal in the natural juices and improve the flavour and colour of the finished dish. The meat is then simmered slowly at a low temperature in liquid, such as water, wine, beer or stock.

POT-ROASTING MEAT

This long, slow method of cooking is ideal for slightly tough joints of meat, such as topside of beef, lamb shoulder and shanks, and knuckle of pork. First, brown the joint over a high heat in a heavy pan or casserole on top of the stove, then remove the joint from the pan. Add chopped or sliced onions, leeks and any root vegetables to the pan, and cook for a few minutes. Replace the meat on top of the vegetables and add a little liquid, such as water, wine, beer or stock. Cover and cook gently in the oven until the meat is tender.

CASSEROLING CHICKEN

Moist cooking methods, such as casseroling, not only bring out the flavour of poultry, they also offer an opportunity to add herbs, spices and aromatics, which will infuse the light meat during the cooking time. Whole birds and joints can be casseroled. First, brown the poultry pieces or bird all over in a large heavy pan or casserole on top of the stove. Remove

CUBING MEAT

TOSSING IN SEASONED FLOUR

BROWNING MEAT

ADDING POT-ROAST INGREDIENTS

CASSEROLING CHICKEN

USING A CAST-IRON TAGINE

the meat from the pan and add chopped onion, carrot, celery and other flavourings to the fat remaining in the pan, and cook until softened. Replace the meat before adding the chosen liquid. Season well, then bring the casserole to simmering point. Cover closely and allow to simmer very gently on top of the stove, or cook, covered, in the oven at 180°C|350°F|Gas 4.

USING A CAST-IRON TAGINE ON A STOVE-TOP

The traditional glazed earthenware tagine can be used only in the oven, but the base of the contemporary cast-iron design can be used on the top of any kind of stove, be it gas, electric or wood-burning, to brown ingredients such as onions, vegetables or meat before the other ingredients are added. Place the cast-iron tagine base on the stove-top, add a little oil and heat. Add the vegetables or meat and cook gently, stirring occasionally, until the ingredients are browned. Add the liquid ingredients, then cover the base and simmer the tagine on top of the stove or in the oven.

MAKING STOCKS

A well-flavoured stock is the basis of good cooking, and if a stock is poor then the resulting soups, casseroles and stews will be poor too. Stocks are not difficult to make but a common mistake is to assume that a stock is made with leftovers. It may have been traditionally, but the way to get a really good stock is to use fresh bones and vegetables. Never add salt until the end of cooking, and always use whole peppercorns because ground pepper will make the stock taste bitter. Fresh herbs or a bouquet garni are essential.

For a basic meat or poultry stock, start by chopping up meat bones or a whole poultry carcass (or ask your butcher to do it for you). Cutting the bones into pieces helps to extract the collagen and impart the maximum possible flavour during cooking. Place the bone or carcass pieces into a large heavy pan and add a quartered onion, sliced celery and carrot, peppercorns and a bouquet garni. Cover with water and bring to the boil, skimming off as much of the scum as possible. Cover the pan and simmer for 2–3 hours, then strain through a sieve into a heatproof bowl. Leave to cool, then chill overnight; the fat will rise to the top and can easily be removed. Heat through to use.

SOUPS

Full of flavour and ideal as a lunch or supper, gently simmered soups are always a popular choice. Fresh ingredients combined with pasta, dried beans and herbs and spices are the basis for many tasty soups. Choose from classics such as Real Old-fashioned Chicken Soup or Bouillabaisse, or opt for a hearty soup such as Chunky Tomato Soup with Noodles or Soup of Toulouse Sausage with Borlotti Beans and Breadcrumbs.

real old-fashioned chicken soup

Ingredients | SERVES 4–6

2kg|4½lb boiling fowl (stewing chicken) with giblets (except liver), or same weight of guinea fowl and chicken wings and thighs, mixed

1 large onion, halved

2 large carrots, halved lengthways

6 celery sticks, roughly chopped

1 bay leaf

175g|6oz vermicelli pasta

45ml|3 tbsp chopped fresh parsley or whole parsley leaves

salt and ground black pepper

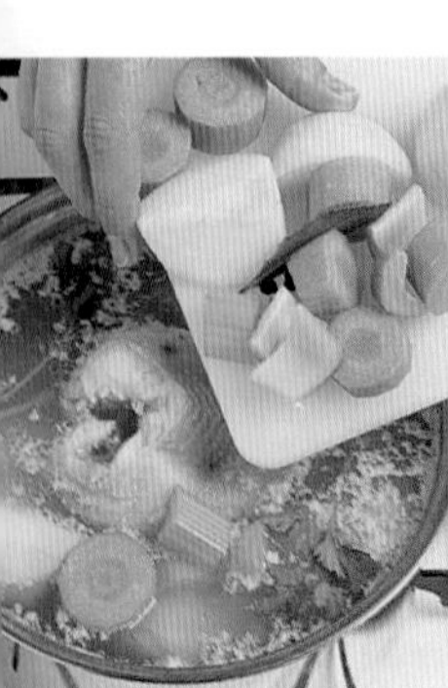

A real chicken soup, clear, golden and warming, filled with lightly cooked pasta, is not called Jewish penicillin for nothing – it really warms you up and it feels as if it is actually doing you good. This one is simmered very gently for at least three hours and then chilled overnight before reheating. Serve as a light lunch or supper dish.

1 Put the chicken, or guinea fowl and chicken pieces, into a large pan with all the vegetables and the bay leaf. Cover with 2.4 litres|4 pints|10 cups cold water. Bring slowly to the boil, skimming off any scum. Add 5ml|1 tsp salt and some ground black pepper.

2 Turn down the heat and simmer the soup slowly for at least 2 hours, or until the fowl is tender. When simmering, the surface of the liquid should just tremble. If it boils, the soup will be cloudy.

3 When tender, remove the bird from the broth and strip the flesh off the carcass. (Allow the meat to cool, then store in the refrigerator for up to 2 days, before using in another recipe.)

4 Return the bones to the soup and simmer very gently for another hour.

5 Strain the soup into a bowl, cool, then chill overnight.

6 The next day the soup should have set to a solid jelly and will be covered with a thin layer of solidified chicken fat. Carefully remove the fat using a spoon.

7 To serve the soup, reheat in a large pan. Add the vermicelli and chopped fresh parsley or whole parsley leaves, and simmer for 6–8 minutes until the pasta is cooked.

8 Taste and season well with plenty of salt and ground black pepper. Serve piping hot.

bouillabaisse

Ingredients | SERVES 4–6

1.3–1.6kg|3–3½lb mixed fish and shellfish, such as red mullet, John Dory, monkfish, large prawns (shrimp) and clams

1.2 litres|2 pints|5 cups water

225g|8oz tomatoes

pinch of saffron threads

90ml|6 tbsp olive oil

1 onion, sliced

1 leek, sliced

1 celery stick, sliced

2 garlic cloves, crushed

bouquet garni

1 strip pared orange rind

2.5ml|½ tsp fennel seeds

15ml|1 tbsp tomato purée (paste)

10ml|2 tsp Pernod

4–6 thick slices French bread

45ml|3 tbsp chopped fresh parsley

salt and ground black pepper

This is perhaps the most famous of all Mediterranean fish soups, originating from Marseilles in the south of France. Aromatic ingredients such as garlic, fennel seeds and saffron are cooked slowly in fish stock before the fish and shellfish are added to the pan.

1 Remove the heads, tails and fins from the fish and put in a large pan, with the water. Bring to the boil, and simmer for 15 minutes. Strain, and reserve the liquid.

2 Cut the fish into large chunks. Leave the shellfish in their shells.

3 Scald the tomatoes, then drain and refresh in cold water. When cool enough to handle, peel and chop them. Soak the saffron in 15–30ml|1–2 tbsp hot water.

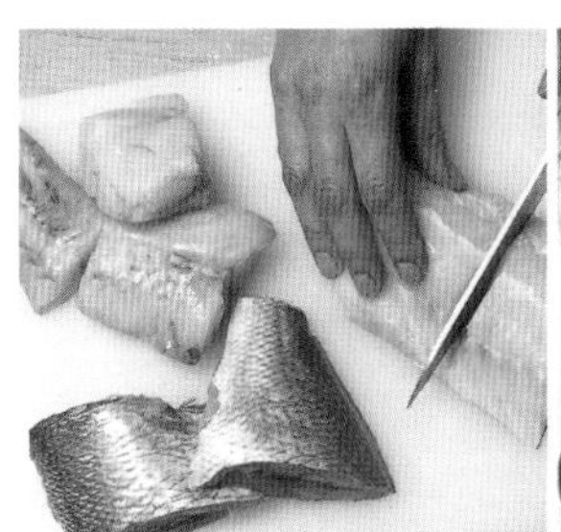

4 Heat the oil in the cleaned large pan, add the onion, leek and celery and cook until softened. Add the garlic, bouquet garni, orange rind, fennel seeds and tomatoes, then stir in the saffron and liquid and the fish stock. Season, then bring to the boil and simmer for 30–40 minutes.

5 Add the shellfish and boil for about 6 minutes. Discard any clams that remain closed. Add the fish and cook for a further 6–8 minutes until it flakes easily. Using a slotted spoon, carefully transfer the fish to a warmed serving platter.

6 Keep the liquid boiling and add the tomato purée and Pernod, then check the seasoning. Place a slice of bread in each soup bowl, pour the broth over and spoon out the fish separately, sprinkled with chopped parsley.

bacon and chickpea soup with tortilla chips

Ingredients | SERVES 4–6

400g|14oz|2 cups dried chickpeas, soaked overnight in cold water then drained

115g|4oz|1/2 cup butter

150g|5oz pancetta or streaky (fatty) bacon, roughly chopped

2 onions, finely chopped

1 carrot, chopped

1 celery stick, chopped

15ml|1 tbsp chopped fresh rosemary

2 bay leaves

2 garlic cloves, halved

salt and ground black pepper

For the Tortilla Chips

75g|3oz|6 tbsp butter

2.5ml|1/2 tsp sweet paprika plus extra to garnish

1.5ml|1/4 tsp ground cumin

175g|6oz plain tortilla chips

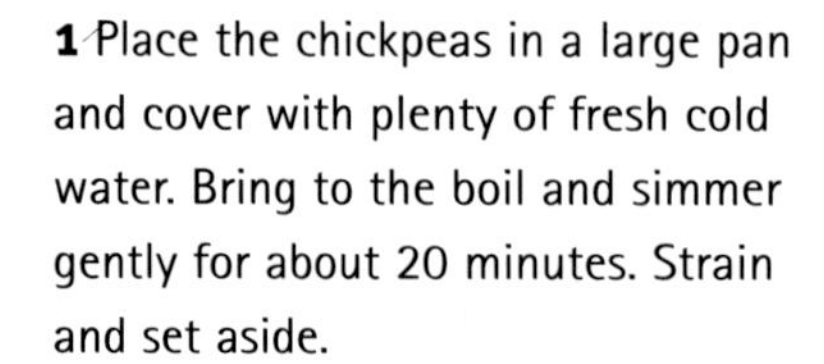

1 Place the chickpeas in a large pan and cover with plenty of fresh cold water. Bring to the boil and simmer gently for about 20 minutes. Strain and set aside.

2 Melt the butter in a large pan and add the pancetta or bacon. Fry over a medium heat until just beginning to turn golden. Add the chopped vegetables and cook for a further 5–10 minutes or until soft.

3 Add the chickpeas to the pan with the chopped rosemary, bay leaves, halved garlic cloves and enough water to cover completely.

4 Bring to the boil, half cover, turn down the heat and simmer for about 45–60 minutes, stirring occasionally. (The chickpeas should start to disintegrate during cooking and will thicken the soup.)

5 Allow the soup to cool slightly, then pour it into a blender or food processor and process until smooth. Return the soup to the rinsed-out pan, taste and season with salt and plenty of black pepper. Reheat gently when ready to serve, until piping hot.

6 To make the spicy tortilla chips, preheat the oven to 180°C|350°F| Gas 4. Melt the butter with the sweet paprika and ground cumin in a pan, then lightly brush the mixture over the tortilla chips. Reserve any left over spiced butter. Spread the chips out in an even layer on a baking sheet and warm through in the oven for 5 minutes.

7 Ladle the hot soup into individual bowls, pour some reserved spiced butter over each serving and sprinkle with a little sweet paprika to garnish. Serve with the warm spicy tortilla chips.

This silky smooth nutty soup is left to gently simmer for up to an hour to allow the flavours to develop. Serve with a bowl of warm and spicy tortilla chips as a TV snack on a cold night.

chunky tomato soup with noodles

Ingredients | SERVES 4

45–60ml|3–4 tbsp olive oil

3–4 cloves

2 onions, chopped

1 butternut squash, peeled, seeded and cut into small chunks

4 celery sticks, chopped

2 carrots, peeled and chopped

8 large, ripe tomatoes, skinned and roughly chopped

5–10ml|1–2 tsp sugar

15ml|1 tbsp tomato purée (paste)

5–10ml|1–2 tsp ras el hanout

2.5ml|½ tsp ground turmeric

a big bunch of fresh coriander (cilantro), chopped (reserve a few sprigs for garnish)

1.75 litres|3 pints|7½ cups vegetable stock

a handful of dried egg noodles or capellini, broken into pieces

salt and ground black pepper

60–75ml|4–5 tbsp creamy yogurt, to serve

A subtly spicy vegetarian soup that is simmered over a low heat with *ras el hanout*, a traditional blend of Moroccan spices. You can purée the soup, if you prefer, but I like it just as it is, finished off with a swirl of yogurt and a sprig of fresh coriander. Garlic lovers may like to add a crushed garlic clove and a little salt to the yogurt. Serve with chunks of fresh bread.

1 In a deep pan, heat the oil and add the cloves, onions, squash, celery and carrots. Fry until they begin to colour, then stir in the tomatoes and sugar. Cook the tomatoes until the water reduces and they begin to pulp.

2 Stir in the tomato purée, *ras el hanout*, turmeric and chopped coriander. Pour in the stock and bring the liquid to the boil. Reduce the heat and simmer for 30–40 minutes until the vegetables are very tender and the liquid has reduced a little.

3 Add the pasta to the liquid in the pan and cook for about 10 minutes until the pasta is soft. Season the soup to taste with salt and pepper and ladle it into warmed bowls.

4 Spoon a swirl of yogurt into each bowl of soup, garnish with fresh coriander and serve with warm bread.

VARIATION

To make a puréed soup, before adding the pasta leave the soup to cool slightly and then process in a food processor or blender.

soup of toulouse sausage with borlotti beans and breadcrumbs

Ingredients | SERVES 6

250g|9oz|generous 1¼ cups borlotti beans, soaked overnight in cold water, then drained

115g|4oz piece pancetta, finely chopped

6 Toulouse sausages, thickly sliced

1 large onion, finely chopped

2 garlic cloves, chopped

2 carrots, finely diced

2 leeks, finely chopped

6 tomatoes, skinned, seeded and chopped

30ml|2 tbsp tomato purée (paste)

1.35 litres|2¼ pints|5⅔ cups vegetable stock

175g|6oz spring greens (collards), shredded

25g|1oz|2 tbsp butter

115g|4oz|2 cups fresh white breadcrumbs

50g|2oz|⅔ cup freshly grated Parmesan cheese

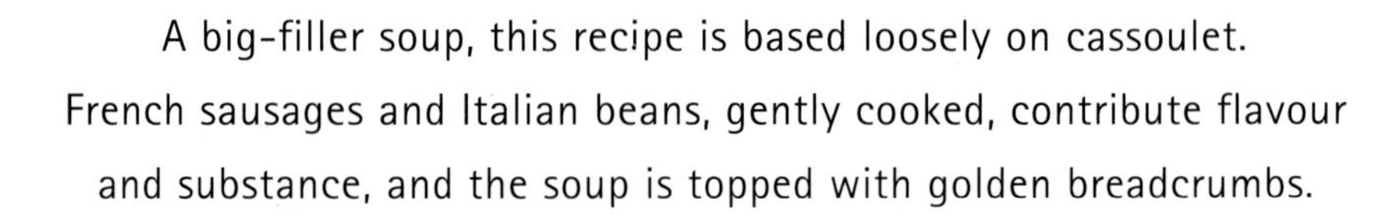

A big-filler soup, this recipe is based loosely on cassoulet. French sausages and Italian beans, gently cooked, contribute flavour and substance, and the soup is topped with golden breadcrumbs.

1 Place the beans in a large pan. Cover with plenty of cold water and bring to the boil, then boil rapidly for 10 minutes. Drain well.

2 Heat a large pan and dry-fry the pancetta until browned and the fat runs. Add the sausages and cook for 4–5 minutes, stirring occasionally, until beginning to brown.

3 Add the onion and garlic to the sausages in the pan and cook for 3–4 minutes until softened. Add the beans, carrots, leeks, tomatoes and tomato purée, then add the stock. Stir, bring to the boil and cover.

4 Simmer for about 1¼ hours or until the beans are tender, then stir in the spring greens and cook for 12–15 minutes more. Season well.

5 Meanwhile, melt the butter in a frying pan and fry the breadcrumbs for 4–5 minutes, stirring, until golden, then stir in the Parmesan.

6 Ladle the soup into six bowls. Sprinkle the fried breadcrumb mixture over each, then serve.

VARIATION

Streaky (fatty) bacon can be used in this recipe in place of the pancetta.

STOVE-TOP CASSEROLES AND STEWS

This tasty selection of one-pot main courses are simple to prepare and can be left to cook and to allow the flavours to develop and then served simply with bread, rice or couscous. Try a traditional North African Tagine of Beef and Peas with Saffron, or the all-in-one Rich Tomato and Chorizo Sauce with Pasta. If you prefer something with a little more kick go for Spicy Chicken Casserole with Red Wine, or Fragrant Lamb Curry.

tagine of beef with peas and saffron

Ingredients | SERVES 6

1.2kg|2½lb chuck steak or braising steak, trimmed and cubed

30ml|2 tbsp olive oil

1 onion, chopped

25g|1oz fresh root ginger, peeled and chopped

5ml|1 tsp ground ginger

pinch of cayenne pepper

pinch of saffron threads

1.2kg|2½ lb shelled fresh peas

2 tomatoes, skinned and chopped

1 preserved lemon, chopped

a handful of brown kalamata olives

salt and ground black pepper

bread or couscous, to serve

1 Put the cubed chuck or braising steak in a tagine, flameproof casserole or heavy pan with the olive oil, chopped onion, fresh and ground ginger, cayenne and saffron and season with salt and pepper.

2 Pour in enough water to cover the meat completely and bring to the boil. Then reduce the heat and cover and simmer for about 1½ hours, or until the meat is very tender. Cook for a little longer if necessary.

3 Add the peas, tomatoes, preserved lemon and olives. Stir well and cook, uncovered, for about 10 minutes, or until the peas are tender and the sauce has reduced. Check the seasoning to taste and serve with bread or plain couscous.

COOK'S TIP

Preserved lemons are a classic North African ingredient. They are stored in salt and can be added to lamb, chicken or vegetable dishes.

This tagine is a popular traditional North African supper dish, and can be made with beef or lamb. The meat is cooked until tender with ginger, cayenne pepper and saffron which imparts a pungent taste and delicate colour. The peas, tomatoes and tangy lemon are added towards the end of cooking to enliven the rich, gingery beef mixture, and the brown olives finish it off.

rich tomato and chorizo sauce with pasta

A pasta sauce should be rich, thick and robust. The assertive flavour of chorizo sausage in this recipe is just delicious combined with tomatoes, red wine and olive oil and simmered for ages.

Ingredients | SERVES 4

225g|8oz fresh chorizo sausage

225g|8oz fresh Italian sausages or good butchers' sausages

30ml|2 tbsp olive oil

1 onion, finely chopped

2 garlic cloves, finely chopped

450ml|¾ pint|scant 2 cups passata (bottled strained tomatoes)

150ml|¼ pint|⅔ cup dry red wine

30ml|2 tbsp tomato purée (paste)

6 sun-dried tomatoes, chopped

15ml|1 tbsp chopped fresh rosemary

30ml|2 tbsp chopped fresh sage

450g|1lb|4 cups dried pasta

salt and ground black pepper

freshly grated Parmesan cheese, for sprinkling

1 Peel off the casing from the chorizo and cut it into even-sized chunks. Process in a blender or food processor until just broken down. Squeeze the sausage meat out of the skins into a bowl and break up the meat. Stir in the processed chorizo.

2 Heat the olive oil in a pan, then add the onion and garlic, and cook for 5 minutes until soft and golden. Stir in the combined sausage meats, browning it all over and breaking up any lumps with a wooden spoon.

3 Pour in the passata and wine, and add the remaining ingredients except the pasta and Parmesan cheese.

4 Stir well and bring to the boil, then turn down the heat, half cover the pan and simmer very gently for at least 1 hour, stirring occasionally, until the oil separates out to form a film on the top and the sauce is reduced.

5 When the sauce is almost ready, cook the pasta in a pan of salted boiling water according to the packet instructions or until just tender, then drain. Season the sauce well and toss with the cooked pasta. Serve sprinkled with the Parmesan cheese.

spicy chicken casserole with red wine

Ingredients | SERVES 4

75ml|5 tbsp extra virgin olive oil

1.6kg|3½lb organic or free-range chicken, jointed

1 large onion, roughly chopped

1 generous glass red wine, about 250ml|8fl oz|1 cup

30ml|2 tbsp tomato purée (paste) diluted in 450ml|¾ pint|scant 2 cups hot water

1 cinnamon stick

3–4 whole allspice

2 bay leaves

salt and ground black pepper

boiled rice, orzo or fried potatoes, to serve

Based on a traditional Greek dish, chicken portions are cooked over a low heat, together with red wine and spices, until succulent. Often served on Sundays and religious festivals, this recipe is served with rice or orzo (small tear-shaped pasta), but for a real treat serve with thick home-made fried potatoes and a simple green salad.

1 Heat the oil in a large pan or sauté pan and brown the chicken pieces on both sides. Lift them out with tongs and set them aside.

2 Add the chopped onion to the hot oil in the pan and stir over a medium heat until it looks translucent.

3 Return the chicken pieces to the pan, pour the wine over and cook for 2–3 minutes, until it has reduced.

4 Add the tomato purée mixture, cinnamon, allspice and bay leaves. Season well, then cover the pan and cook gently for 1 hour or until the chicken is tender. Serve with rice, orzo or fried potatoes.

COOK'S TIPS

- If you can, use organic or free-range chicken for a better flavour.
- If you prefer to cook the casserole in the oven, preheat it to 180°C|350°F|Gas 4 and cook for 45–60 minutes or until the chicken is cooked right through and tender.
- Whole allspice berries are used to flavour this dish. They are dried, unripe berries and have a warm spicy flavour which is similar to a combination of nutmeg, cinnamon and cloves. If you can't get hold of allspice, 5ml|1 tsp ground allspice can be used instead.

spiced lamb with tomatoes and peppers

Ingredients | SERVES 6

1.5kg | 3¼lb lean boneless lamb, cubed

250ml | 8fl oz | 1 cup natural (plain) yogurt

30ml | 2 tbsp sunflower oil

3 onions

2 red (bell) peppers, seeded and cut into chunks

3 garlic cloves, finely chopped

1 red chilli, seeded and chopped

2.5cm | 1in piece fresh root ginger, peeled and chopped

30ml | 2 tbsp mild curry paste

2 x 400g | 14oz cans chopped tomatoes

large pinch of saffron threads

800g | 1¾lb plum tomatoes, halved, seeded and cut into chunks

salt and ground black pepper

chopped fresh coriander (cilantro), to garnish

Lean tender lamb from the leg is gently cooked for this lightly spiced curry with succulent peppers and wedges of onion. Serve warm naan bread to mop up the tomato-rich juices.

1 Mix the lamb with the yogurt in a bowl. Cover and chill for about 1 hour. (Marinating in yogurt tenderizes the meat and reduces the cooking time.)

2 Heat the oil in a wok or large pan. Drain the lamb and reserve the yogurt, then cook the lamb in batches until it is golden brown on all sides. Remove from the pan and set aside.

3 Cut two of the onions into wedges (six from each onion) and add to the oil remaining in the pan.

4 Fry the onion wedges for about 10 minutes. Add the peppers and cook for a further 5 minutes. Remove the vegetables from the pan and set aside.

5 Meanwhile, chop the remaining onion. Add it to the oil in the pan with the garlic, chilli and ginger, and cook, stirring often, until softened.

6 Stir in the curry paste and canned tomatoes with the reserved yogurt marinade. Replace the lamb, season and stir well. Bring to the boil, reduce the heat and simmer for 30 minutes.

7 Pound the saffron to a powder in a mortar, stir in boiling water to dissolve the saffron and add to the curry. Replace the onion and pepper mixture. Stir in the fresh tomatoes and bring back to simmering point, then cook for 15 minutes. Garnish and serve.

fragrant lamb curry

Ingredients | SERVES 4

1 large onion, roughly chopped
10ml|2 tsp grated fresh root ginger
10ml|2 tsp crushed garlic
4–5 garlic cloves
2.5ml|1/2 tsp black peppercorns
6 green cardamom pods
5cm|2in piece cinnamon stick, halved
8 lamb rib chops
60ml|4 tbsp vegetable oil
1 large onion, finely sliced
175ml|6fl oz|3/4 cup natural (plain) yogurt
50g|2oz|1/4 cup butter
2.5ml|1/2 tsp salt
2.5ml|1/2 tsp ground cumin
2.5ml|1/2 tsp hot chilli powder
2.5ml|1/2 tsp freshly grated nutmeg
2.5ml|1/2 tsp granulated sugar
15ml|1 tbsp lime juice
pinch of saffron threads, steeped in 15ml|1 tbsp hot water for 10–15 minutes
15ml|1 tbsp rose water
rose petals, to garnish

1 Process the chopped onion in a blender or food processor. Add a little water, if necessary, to form a purée.

2 Put the purée in a glass bowl and add the grated ginger, crushed garlic, cloves, peppercorns, cardamom pods and cinnamon stick. Mix well.

3 Put the lamb chops in a large shallow glass dish and add the spice mixture. Mix thoroughly, cover the bowl and leave the lamb to marinate for 3–4 hours or overnight in the refrigerator. Bring back to room temperature before cooking.

4 In a wok or large pan, heat the oil and fry the onion until golden brown. Remove the onion with a slotted spoon, squeezing out as much oil as possible. Drain on kitchen paper.

5 In the remaining oil, fry the marinated lamb chops for 5 minutes, stirring frequently. Reduce the heat to low, cover and cook for 5–7 minutes.

6 Meanwhile, mix the yogurt and butter together in a pan and place over a low heat. Cook for 5 minutes, stirring, then stir into the lamb chops along with the salt. Add the cumin and chilli powder and cover the pan. Cook for 45 minutes until the chops are tender.

7 Add the nutmeg and sugar, cook for 1–2 minutes, and then add the lime juice, saffron and rose water. Stir and mix well, simmer for 2–3 minutes and remove from the heat. Garnish with the fried onion and rose petals. Serve with naan bread or boiled basmati rice, if you like.

A delicious curry from Bengal in eastern India. Lamb rib chops are marinated in an aromatic spice mixture and then gently cooked with yogurt, chilli and cumin. Sprinkle fried onion and rose petals over the top and serve with naan bread or basmati rice.

veal in a wheat beer sauce with onions and carrots

The slight bitterness that the wheat beer gives the sauce in this delectable stew is matched by the sweetness of the caramelized onions and carrots.

Ingredients | SERVES 4

45ml|3 tbsp plain (all-purpose) flour, seasoned

900g|2lb boned shoulder or leg of veal cut into 5cm|2in cubes

65g|2½ oz|5 tbsp butter

3 shallots, finely chopped

1 celery stick

fresh parsley sprig

2 fresh bay leaves

5ml|1 tsp caster (superfine) sugar, plus a good pinch

200ml|7fl oz|scant 1 cup wheat beer

450ml|¾ pint|scant 2 cups veal stock

20–25 large silverskin onions or small pickling onions

450g|1lb carrots, thickly sliced

2 large egg yolks

105ml|7 tbsp double (heavy) cream

a little lemon juice (optional)

30ml|2 tbsp chopped fresh parsley

salt and ground black pepper

1 Dust the veal in the flour. Heat 25g|1 oz|2 tbsp butter in a deep, lidded frying pan, add the veal and seal on all sides. Set aside.

2 Add another 15g|½ oz|1 tbsp butter to the pan. Cook the shallots.

3 Replace the veal. Tie the celery, parsley and 1 bay leaf together in a bundle, then add to the pan with a good pinch of caster sugar.

4 Increase the heat, pour in the beer and pour on the stock. Season, bring to the boil, then cover and simmer, stirring once or twice, for 50 minutes.

5 Meanwhile, melt the remaining butter in another frying pan and fry the onions until golden. Remove from the pan and set aside.

6 Add the carrots and turn to coat them in the butter remaining from the onions. Stir in 15ml|1 tsp caster sugar, a pinch of salt, the remaining bay leaf and water to cover the carrots. Bring to the boil and cook for 10 minutes.

7 Return the onions to the pan with the carrots and cook until slightly caramelized. Keep warm. Transfer the veal to a bowl and discard the celery and herb bundle.

8 Beat the egg yolks and cream, then beat in a ladleful of the carrot liquid. Heat in the deep, lidded pan, stirring, until the sauce is thickened.

9 Add the veal, carrots, and onions and heat through. Season to taste, add a little lemon juice, if using, and serve sprinkled with chopped parsley.

OVEN ROASTS AND BAKES

Slowly simmered oven-cooked dishes, with aromatic herbs, spices and vegetables, have a delicious flavour all of their own. Choose from traditional dishes such as Beef Hotpot with Dumplings or Steak and Mushroom Suet Pudding. Or for classics with a twist try Roast Chicken with Potatoes and Lemon or Pot-roast Pork with Apple. Tagine of Yam, Carrots and Prunes or Leek, Squash and Tomato Gratin are ideal as vegetarian main or side dishes.

beef hotpot with herb dumplings

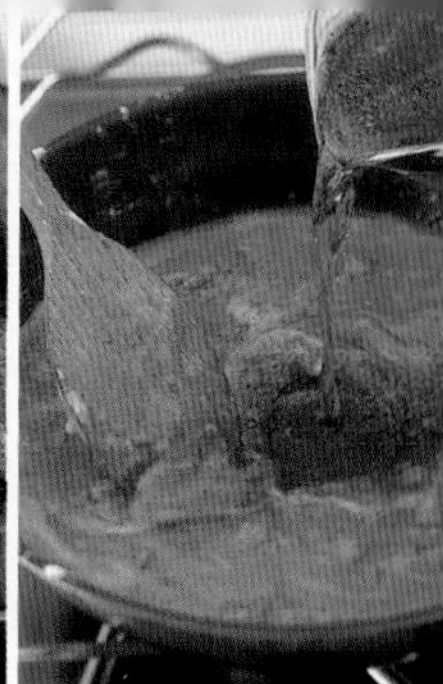

Tender chunks of beef braised in beer, flavoured with shallots and mushrooms and served with parsley and thyme dumplings.

1 Place the porcini mushrooms in a bowl, add the warm water and leave to soak. In a frying pan, melt half the butter with half the oil, add the lardons or pancetta and quickly brown. Remove with a slotted spoon and transfer to the casserole.

2 Add the beef to the frying pan and brown in batches, then, using a slotted spoon, transfer to the casserole. Sprinkle the flour into the fat remaining in the frying pan and stir in well.

3 Stir the beer and beef stock into the flour and bring to the boil, stirring constantly. Strain the mushroom soaking liquid and add to the frying pan, along with the porcini mushrooms. Season well. Pour the sauce over the meat, then add the bouquet garni.

4 Cover the casserole and place in an unheated oven. Set the oven to 200°C|400°F|Gas 6. Cook for about 30 minutes, then reduce the oven temperature to 160°C|325°F|Gas 3 and cook for a further 1 hour.

5 Heat the remaining butter and oil in a frying pan and cook the shallots until golden. Remove and set aside. Add the button mushrooms and sauté for 2–3 minutes. Stir the shallots and mushrooms into the casserole and cook for 30 minutes.

6 In a large bowl, mix together the dumpling ingredients with sufficient cold water to bind to a soft, sticky dough. Divide into 12 and use your hands to form into small balls. Place on top of the hotpot, then cover and cook for 25 minutes more. Serve straight from the casserole.

Ingredients | SERVES 4

20g|¾oz|⅓ cup dried porcini mushrooms
60ml|4 tbsp warm water
40g|1½oz|3 tbsp butter
30ml|2 tbsp sunflower oil
115g|4oz|⅔ cup lardons or cubed pancetta
900g|2lb lean braising steak, cut into chunks
45ml|3 tbsp plain (all-purpose) flour
450ml|¾ pint|scant 2 cups beer
450ml|¾ pint|scant 2 cups beef stock
bouquet garni
8 shallots
175g|6oz|2 cups button (white) mushrooms
salt and ground black pepper
sprigs of thyme, to garnish

For the Herb Dumplings

115g|4oz|1 cup self-raising (self-rising) flour
50g|2oz|scant ½ cup shredded suet
2.5ml|½ tsp salt
2.5ml|½ tsp mustard powder
15ml|1 tbsp chopped fresh parsley
15ml|1 tbsp chopped fresh thyme

steak and mushroom pudding with a herby suet crust

Tender stewed steak and mushrooms are wrapped in a herby suet pastry to make this wonderful British classic. Serve with creamy mashed potatoes and carrots for a traditional meal.

Ingredients | SERVES 6

1.3kg|3lb rump (round) steak, trimmed and cubed

30ml|2 tbsp plain (all-purpose) flour

30ml|2 tbsp olive or sunflower oil

1 large onion, chopped

25g|1oz|1/2 cup dried porcini mushrooms, soaked in warm water for 20 minutes, drained and roughly chopped

225g|8oz chestnut mushrooms, halved

300ml|1/2 pint|1 1/4 cups fruity red wine

300ml|1/2 pint|1 1/4 cups beef stock

45ml|3 tbsp mushroom ketchup (optional)

salt and ground black pepper

1 bay leaf

For the Herby Suet Crust

275g|10oz|2 1/2 cups self-raising (self-rising) flour

5ml|1 tsp baking powder

15ml|1 tbsp each finely chopped fresh parsley, sage, rosemary and thyme

finely grated rind of 1 lemon

75g|3oz|1/2 cup beef or vegetable suet

50g|2oz|1/4 cup butter, chilled and grated

1 egg, beaten

juice of 1/2 lemon

150ml|1/4 pint|2/3 cup cold water

1 Preheat the oven to 180°C|350°F|Gas 4. Toss the steak in plain flour and season. Heat the oil in a frying pan, cook the onion, then transfer to a casserole. Fry the steak until browned.

2 Stir the meat into the casserole with both types of mushrooms. Pour in the soaking liquid, wine, stock, mushroom ketchup, if using, and the bay leaf. Cover and cook for 1 1/2 hours, until the meat is tender. Allow to cool.

3 For the herby suet crust, butter a 1.75 litre|3 pint|7 1/2 cup bowl. Sift the flour, baking powder and 2.5ml|1/2 tsp salt into a mixing bowl. Stir in the herbs and lemon rind and season. Stir in the suet and butter and make a well in the centre. Add the egg, lemon juice and enough cold water to mix. Gather into a soft, manageable dough.

4 Knead the dough, then cut off a quarter and wrap in clear film (plastic wrap). Shape the rest into a ball and roll into a round, big enough to line the casserole. Lift up the dough and drop it into the casserole. Roll out the reserved pastry to use as a lid.

5 Spoon in the beef filling to within 1cm|1/2in of the rim and top up with gravy. Dampen the edges of the pastry and fit the lid, pressing the edges to seal and trimming the excess. Cover with pleated, buttered baking parchment; tie with string to hold in place, cover with pleated foil and tie string over the top to form a handle.

6 Place the bowl in a large pan of simmering water, cover and steam for 1 1/2 hours. Serve the pudding straight from the bowl.

roast chicken with potatoes and lemon

Ingredients | SERVES 4

1 organic or free-range chicken, about 1.6kg | $3\frac{1}{2}$lb

2 garlic cloves, peeled but left whole

15ml | 1 tbsp chopped fresh, or 5ml | 1 tsp dried, thyme or oregano, plus 2–3 fresh thyme or oregano sprigs

800g | $1\frac{3}{4}$lb potatoes

juice of 1 lemon

60ml | 4 tbsp extra virgin olive oil

300ml | $\frac{1}{2}$ pint | $1\frac{1}{4}$ cups hot water

salt and ground black pepper

crisp, leafy salad, to serve

Based on a traditional Greek recipe this is a lovely, easy dish for a family meal. Everything is roasted together so that the potatoes and chicken absorb all the different flavours, especially that of the lemon.

1 Preheat the oven to 200°C | 400°F | Gas 6. Place the chicken, breast side down, in a large roasting pan, then tuck the garlic cloves and the thyme or oregano sprigs inside the bird.

2 Peel the potatoes and quarter them lengthways. If they are very large, slice them lengthways into thinner pieces. Arrange the potatoes around the chicken, then pour the lemon juice over the chicken and potatoes. Season with salt and pepper.

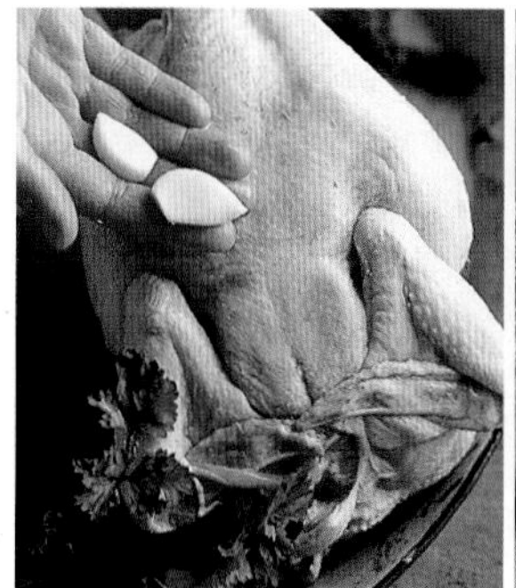

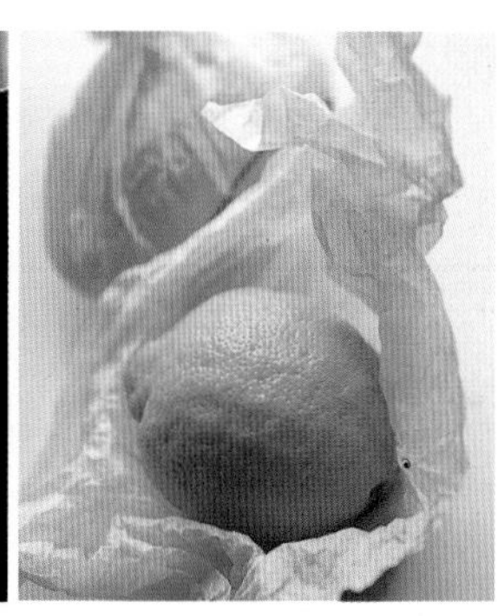

3 Drizzle the olive oil over the top of the chicken and add three-quarters of the chopped fresh or dried thyme or oregano. Pour the hot water into the roasting pan.

4 Roast the chicken and potatoes for 30 minutes, then remove the roasting pan from the oven and carefully turn the chicken over.

5 Season the bird, sprinkle over the remaining fresh or dried herbs, and add more hot water, if needed. Reduce the oven temperature to 190°C | 375°F | Gas 5.

6 Return the chicken and potatoes to the oven and roast them for another hour, or slightly longer, by which time both the chicken and the potatoes will be a golden brown colour. Serve simply with a crisp leafy salad.

pot-roast loin of pork with apple

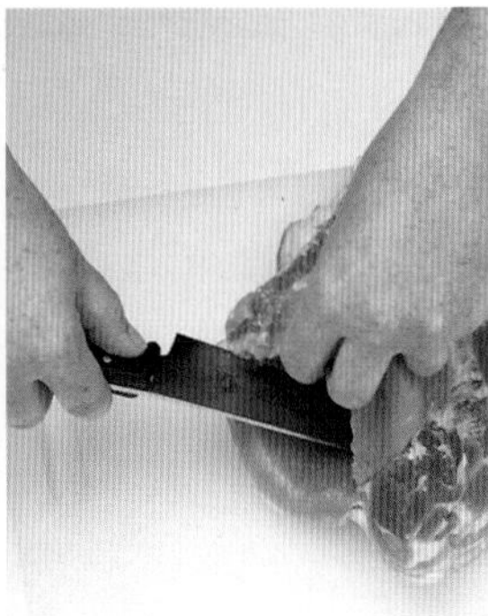

Ingredients | SERVES 6–8

1.8kg|4lb boned loin of pork

300ml|1/2 pint|1 1/4 cups dry (hard) cider

150ml|1/4 pint|2/3 cup sour cream

7.5ml|1 1/2 tsp salt

For the Stuffing

25g|1oz|2 tbsp butter

1 small onion, chopped

50g|2oz|1 cup fresh white breadcrumbs

2 apples, cored, peeled and chopped

50g|2oz|scant 1/2 cup raisins

finely grated rind of 1 orange

pinch of ground cloves

salt and ground black pepper

1 Preheat the oven to 220°C|425°F|Gas 7. To make the fruity stuffing, first melt the butter in a pan and fry the onion until soft. In a bowl, mix the breadcrumbs, chopped apple, raisins, orange rind and ground cloves. Add the onion and season well.

2 Put the pork, rind side down, on a board. Make a horizontal cut between the meat and outer layer of fat, cutting to within 2.5cm|1in of the edges to make a pocket.

3 Push the stuffing into the pocket. Roll up the pork lengthways and tie with string. Score the rind at 2cm|3/4in intervals with a sharp knife.

4 Pour the cider and sour cream into a large casserole. Stir to combine, then add the pork, rind side down. Transfer to the oven and cook, uncovered, for 30 minutes.

5 Turn the joint over, so that the rind is on top. Baste, then sprinkle with salt. Cook for a further 1 hour, basting after 30 minutes. Reduce the oven temperature to 180°C|350°F|Gas 4. Cook for 1 1/2 hours, then remove the casserole from the oven and leave to stand for 20 minutes before carving.

Cook's Tip

Do not baste the meat during the final 1 1/2 hours of roasting, so that the crackling becomes crisp.

Roasted pork loin gently cooked in a creamy cider sauce with traditional crispy crackling and a lightly spiced apple and raisin stuffing makes a wonderful main course for Sunday lunch.

butter bean cassoulet

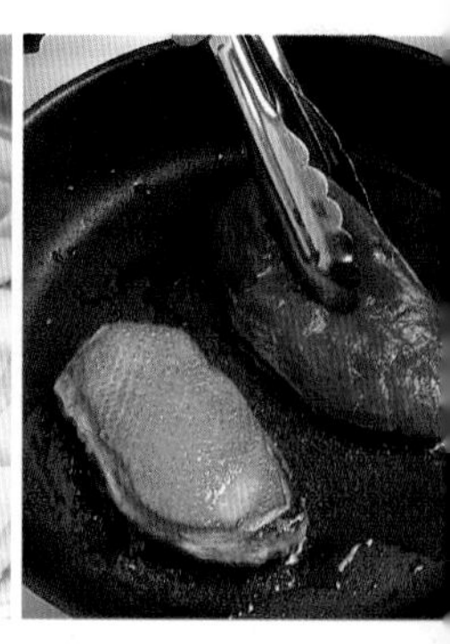

Cassoulet is peasant food originating from the south-west of France. It is a very hearty, one-pot meal of white beans, preserved meats and sausage. The beans are simmered gently with herbs and flavourings, and then the duck and sausage are added towards the end of cooking.

Ingredients | SERVES 6–8

675g | 1½lb | 3¾ cups dried butter (lima) beans, soaked overnight in cold water, then drained

2 large onions, sliced

6 large garlic cloves, crushed

3 bay leaves

10ml | 2 tsp dried thyme

2 whole cloves

60ml | 4 tbsp tomato purée (paste)

12 sun-dried tomatoes in oil, drained and roughly chopped

450g | 1lb smoked pancetta in a piece

60ml | 4 tbsp olive oil

4 boneless duck breast portions

12 Toulouse or chunky Italian sausages

400g | 14oz can plum tomatoes

75g | 3oz | 1½ cups stale white breadcrumbs

salt and ground black pepper

crusty bread, to serve

1 Tip the drained beans into a large pan. Cover with fresh water and bring to the boil. Boil rapidly for 10 minutes, then drain well and tip into a large flameproof casserole. Add the sliced onions, crushed garlic, bay leaves, dried thyme, whole cloves, tomato purée and drained and roughly chopped sun-dried tomatoes.

2 Trim the rind from the smoked pancetta and cut into large even-sized pieces. Heat about 30ml | 2 tbsp of the olive oil in a frying pan and brown the pancetta pieces in several batches.

3 Stir it into the casserole and add enough cold water to cover. Bring to the boil, then reduce the heat so that it just simmers. Cover and simmer the cassoulet for about 1½ hours until the beans are tender.

4 Preheat the oven to 180°C | 350°F | Gas 4. Score the skin of the duck. Heat the remaining oil in a frying pan and fry the duck, skin side down, until golden brown. Cut each breast portion into large even-sized pieces, then transfer to the casserole. Cut each sausage into three.

5 Lightly fry the sausages in the fat remaining in the frying pan, then stir into the beans with the canned tomatoes, adding salt and ground black pepper to taste.

6 Sprinkle the white breadcrumbs in an even layer over the surface of the cassoulet and bake in the oven for 45–60 minutes, or until a golden brown crust has formed on the surface. Serve warm with crusty bread to mop up all the sauce.

tagine of yam, carrots and prunes

Ingredients | SERVES 4–6

45ml|3 tbsp olive oil

a little butter

25–30 pearl or button onions, blanched and peeled

900g|2lb yam or sweet potatoes, peeled and cut into bitesize chunks

2–3 carrots, cut into bitesize chunks

150g|5oz|generous ½ cup ready-to-eat pitted prunes

5ml|1 tsp ground cinnamon

2.5ml|½ tsp ground ginger

10ml|2 tsp clear honey

450ml|¾ pint|scant 2 cups vegetable stock

small bunch of fresh coriander (cilantro), finely chopped

small bunch of mint, finely chopped

salt and ground black pepper

The vegetables in this succulent, syrupy tagine should be slightly caramelized. They are at their best served with couscous or lots of warm, crusty bread and a leafy, herb-filled salad.

1 Preheat the oven to 200°C|400°F|Gas 6. Heat the olive oil in a casserole with the butter.

2 Stir in the peeled onions and cook for about 5 minutes, until the onions are tender, then remove half the onions from the pan and set aside.

3 Add the yam or sweet potatoes and carrots to the pan and cook until lightly browned. Stir in the prunes with the cinnamon, ginger and honey.

4 Pour in the stock and season well with salt and ground black pepper. Cover the casserole and transfer to the oven for about 45 minutes.

5 Stir in the reserved onions and bake for a further 10 minutes. Gently stir in the fresh coriander and mint, and serve the tagine immediately.

COOK'S TIP

The yam has a brown skin and cream-coloured flesh; the sweet potato has dark red or orange skin and orange flesh. Buy firm specimens that do not "give" when pressed.

leek, squash and tomato gratin

Ingredients | SERVES 4–6

450g | 1lb peeled and seeded squash, cut into 1cm | 1/2in slices

60ml | 4 tbsp olive oil

450g | 1lb leeks, cut into thick, diagonal slices

675g | 1 1/2lb tomatoes, skinned and thickly sliced

2.5ml | 1/2 tsp ground toasted cumin seeds

450ml | 3/4 pint | scant 2 cups single (light) cream

1 fresh red chilli, seeded and thinly sliced

1 garlic clove, finely chopped

15ml | 1 tbsp chopped fresh mint

30ml | 2 tbsp chopped fresh parsley

60ml | 4 tbsp fine white breadcrumbs

salt and ground black pepper

This autumnal gratin complements roast or grilled lamb or chicken. Or serve it as a simple all-in-one supper dish accompanied by a green salad and good bread.

1 Steam the squash slices over boiling salted water for 10 minutes.

2 Heat half the oil in a frying pan and cook the leeks gently for 5 minutes until lightly coloured. Try to keep the slices intact. Preheat the oven to 190°C | 375°F | Gas 5.

3 Layer the squash, leek and tomato slices in a 2 litre | 3 1/2 pint | 8 cup gratin dish, arranging them in rows. Season well with salt, ground black pepper and cumin.

4 Heat the cream in a small pan with the chilli and garlic. Bring to the boil, then stir in the mint and pour over the vegetables, thoroughly scraping the contents out of the pan.

5 Bake for 50–55 minutes, or until the gratin is bubbling and the vegetables are tender. Sprinkle the parsley and breadcrumbs on top and drizzle over the remaining oil. Then bake for another 15–20 minutes until the breadcrumbs are browned and crisp. Serve immediately.

PUDDINGS AND DESSERTS

Simple puds that can be cooked in advance or just popped in the oven really are the best! Sticky Maple and Pecan Steamed Pud is a deliciously indulgent treat on a cold winter's day. Or make the most of autumn fruit and try Spiced Pears with Nut Crumble. For a wicked chocolate dessert to impress serve Hazelnut Pain au Chocolat Pudding, or for an updated dinner party classic try fragrant Saffron and Cardamom Crème Caramel.

sticky maple and pecan steamed pud

Ingredients | SERVES 6

60ml|4 tbsp maple syrup

30ml|2 tbsp fresh brown breadcrumbs

115g|4oz|1 cup shelled pecan nuts, roughly chopped

115g|4oz|1/2 cup butter, softened

finely grated rind of 1 orange

115g|4oz|heaped 1/2 cup golden caster (superfine) sugar

2 eggs, beaten

175g|6oz|1 1/2 cups self-raising (self-rising) flour, sifted

pinch of salt

about 75ml|5 tbsp milk

extra maple syrup and home-made custard or double (heavy) cream, to serve

1 Butter a 900ml|1 1/2 pint|3 3/4 cup heatproof bowl generously. Stir the maple syrup, breadcrumbs and roughly chopped pecan nuts together and spoon into the bowl.

2 Cream the butter with the orange rind and sugar until light and fluffy. Gradually beat in the eggs, then fold in the flour and salt. Stir in enough milk to make a loose mixture that will drop off the spoon if lightly shaken.

3 Carefully spoon the sponge mixture into the prepared bowl, on top of the syrup and nuts.

4 Cover the sponge with pleated, buttered baking parchment, then with pleated foil (the pleats allow for expansion during cooking). Tie string under the lip of the bowl to hold the paper in place, then take it over the top to form a handle.

5 Place the bowl in a large pan of simmering water, cover and steam for 2 hours, topping up with boiling water as necessary.

6 Turn out the pudding on to a serving plate. Serve with extra maple syrup and custard or double cream.

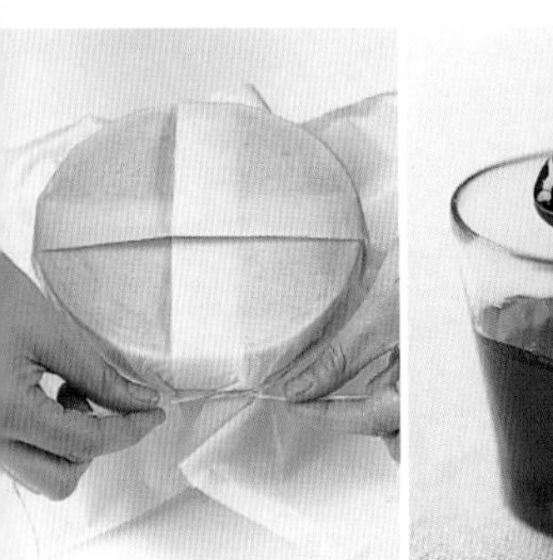

Imagine a hot sponge cake, straight out of the oven but with a less golden crust, a deeper sponge and more crumbliness – that's a steamed pudding. It can be flavoured with anything – maple syrup and pecan nuts are wonderful, and look superb when turned out, as here. Serve with lots of your own home-made custard.

spiced pears with nut crumble

Ingredients | SERVES 4–6

900g|2lb pears
30ml|2 tbsp lemon juice
40g|1½oz|3 tbsp caster (superfine) sugar
5ml|1 tsp mixed (apple pie) spice
2.5ml|½ tsp grated nutmeg

FOR THE CRUMBLE TOPPING

75g|3oz|⅔ cup plain (all-purpose) flour
75g|3oz|6 tbsp butter
50g|2oz|¼ cup light muscovado (brown) sugar
50g|2oz|½ cup pecan nuts or walnuts, chopped
40g|1½oz|scant ½ cup rolled oats
vanilla ice cream or double (heavy) cream, to serve

An all-time favourite, this crumble has a crunchy nut and oat topping, which complements the slowly baked spicy pears hidden beneath.

1 Soak a small terracotta pot in cold water for 15 minutes, then drain. Peel the pears if wished, then halve them and remove the cores. Cut each pear into six wedges and toss in the lemon juice to coat.

2 Place the pears in the clay pot, add the sugar, mixed spice and nutmeg and mix together.

3 Cover and place the pot in an unheated oven. Set the oven to 200°C|400°F|Gas 6 and cook the pears for 25 minutes.

4 Meanwhile, prepare the crumble topping. Sift the flour into a bowl and rub in the butter, then stir in the sugar, nuts and rolled oats.

5 Uncover the clay pot and stir gently to rearrange the fruit in the pot. Spoon the nut and oat crumble mixture over the pears.

6 Return the clay pot to the oven for a further 25–30 minutes, or until the crumble topping is golden brown. Serve the crumble warm, with vanilla ice cream or double cream.

COOK'S TIP
Look out for the golden-skinned Forelle pears, which are especially good for cooking, or try Anjou, Williams or Conference pears.

hazelnut pain au chocolat pudding

Ingredients | SERVES 6

4 large pains au chocolat

75g|3oz chocolate and hazelnut spread

For the Custard

300ml|1/2 pint|1 1/4 cups milk

300ml|1/2 pint|1 1/4 cups double (heavy) cream

1 vanilla pod (bean), split

6 egg yolks

115g|4oz|heaped 1/2 cup caster (superfine) sugar

icing (confectioners') sugar, for dusting

pouring cream, to serve

1 Butter a 1.75 litre|3 pint|7 1/2 cup shallow baking dish. Cut the pains au chocolat into thick slices, then spread them with the chocolate and hazelnut spread. Arrange the slices, spread side up and overlapping, in the prepared greased dish.

2 To make the custard, pour the milk and double cream into a pan. Add the split vanilla pod and place over a very low heat for 5 minutes until the mixture is almost boiling and well flavoured with vanilla.

3 Meanwhile, in a large bowl, whisk together the egg yolks and caster sugar until light and creamy. Strain the flavoured milk on to the egg mixture, whisking well. Pour the egg mixture evenly over the pains au chocolat.

4 Allow to stand for 10 minutes to allow the pains au chocolat to absorb the liquid. Preheat the oven to 180°C|350°F|Gas 4.

5 Place the baking dish in a large roasting pan and pour in enough boiling water to come halfway up the sides of the dish. Bake the pudding for 45–50 minutes until the custard is softly set and the top is crisp and golden brown.

6 Remove from the oven and leave the pudding in the roasting pan of water until just warm. Sprinkle with the icing sugar and serve with cream.

VARIATION

If using plain croissants, just spread with extra chocolate spread in step 1.

This is a wickedly decadent version of classic bread and butter pudding, and it is equally at home as an informal indulgence or as a real dinner party treat. The ingredients are simply combined and then gently baked in a *bain marie* (or water bath) to ensure the pudding is not overcooked. The result is a chocolate treat to die for!

saffron and cardamom crème caramel with butter cookies

Baked in the oven until just set and then chilled overnight, these crème caramels are a deliciously fragrant version of a classic dessert. Serve with crisp butter cookies flavoured with orange flower water.

Ingredients | SERVES 4

600ml|1 pint|2½ cups milk

115g|4oz|⅔ cup sugar, plus 60ml|4 tbsp for caramel

pinch of saffron threads

2.5ml|½ tsp cardamom seeds

15–30ml|1–2 tbsp rose water

4 eggs, lightly beaten

60ml|4 tbsp boiling water

For the Cookies

200g|7oz|scant 1 cup butter

130g|4½oz|generous 1 cup icing (confectioners') sugar, sifted

5–10ml|1–2 tsp orange flower water

250g|9oz|2¼ cups plain (all-purpose) flour, sifted

handful of blanched almonds

1 Preheat the oven to 180°C|350°F|Gas 4. Heat the milk, sugar, saffron and cardamom in a pan until the milk is just about to boil. Set aside to cool. Add the rose water, then gradually pour the mixture into the eggs, beating constantly. Set aside.

2 To make the caramel, heat the 60ml|4 tbsp sugar in a small heavy pan until melted. Stir in the water, holding the pan at arm's length as the caramel will spit. Let it bubble before tipping it into four dishes, swirling to coat the base and sides evenly. Cool.

3 Pour the custard into the dishes and stand them in a roasting pan. Pour in cold water to two-thirds of the way up the dishes. Bake in the oven for 1 hour, or until set. Cool, then chill for several hours or overnight.

4 To make the cookies, melt the butter in a pan and leave to cool until lukewarm. Stir in the icing sugar and orange flower water, then gradually beat in the flour to form a smooth, stiff dough. Wrap in clear film (plastic wrap) and chill for 15 minutes.

5 Preheat the oven to 180°C|350°F|Gas 4. Grease a baking sheet. Break off walnut-sized pieces of dough and roll into balls. Place on the baking sheet and flatten slightly. Press a nut into the centre of each. Bake for 20 minutes, or until golden. Allow to cool slightly on the baking sheet; when firm, transfer to a wire rack.

6 To serve, run a knife around the edges of the crème caramel dishes and invert on to plates. Serve with the cookies.

index